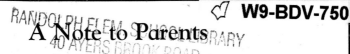
☑ **W9-BDV-750**

A Note to Parents

Dorling Kindersley *Readers* is a compelling new program for beginning readers, designed in conjunction with leading literacy experts, including Dr. Linda Gambrell, President of the National Reading Conference and past board member of the International Reading Association.

Beautiful illustrations and superb full-color photographs combine with engaging, easy-to-read stories to offer a fresh approach to each subject in the series. Each Dorling Kindersley *Reader* is guaranteed to capture a child's interest while developing his or her reading skills, general knowledge, and love of reading.

The four levels of Dorling Kindersley *Readers* are aimed at different reading abilities, enabling you to choose the books that are exactly right for your child:

Level 1 for **Preschool to Grade 1**
Level 2 for **Grades 1 to 3**
Level 3 for **Grades 2 and 3**
Le

Dorling **DK** Kindersley

LONDON, NEW YORK, SYDNEY, DELHI, PARIS,
MUNICH and JOHANNESBURG

Produced by NFL Publishing Group
Vice-President/Editor in Chief
John Wiebusch
Managing Editor Chuck Garrity, Sr.
Project Editor James Buckley, Jr.
Art Director Bill Madrid
Designer Helen Choy Whang

For DK Publishing
Editor Regina Kahney
Reading Consultant
Linda Gambrell, Ph.D.

First American Edition, 2000
Published in the United States by
Dorling Kindersley, Inc.
95 Madison Ave., New York, NY 10016

2 4 6 8 10 9 7 5 3 1

Library of Congress Catalog #00-024794

ISBN 0-7894-6376-8 (hc)
ISBN 0-7894-6759-3 (pb)

Printed in China

All Photographs are Copyright © NFL Photos.
l=left, r=right; FC=front cover   •
Peter Brouillet: FC, 28, 43; Michael Burr: 19, 31; Scott
Cunningham: 42; Bruce Dierdorff: 25; Dorling
Kindersley: 15; Brian Drake: 18; David Drapkin: 26;
Dan Honda: 36; Paul Jasienski: 30; David Lesson: 14;
Al Messerschmidt: 24, 32; Peter Read Miller: 38; Ron
Modra: 4; Roger Motzkus (illus.): 8; NFL Photos: 6, 20,
33, 44, 45, 47; NFL Photos/Aikman Family: 7, 10; NFL
Photos/Kevin Terrell: 16; Bob Rosato: 16; James D.
Smith: 21, 22, 34r, 35, 46; Al Tielmans: 34l;
Tony Tomsic: FC; Baron Wolman: 39.

see our complete
catalog at
www.dk.com

Contents

DORLING KINDERSLEY READERS

READING
3
ALONE

TROY AIKMAN
CHAMPIONSHIP QUARTERBACK

Written by James Buckley, Jr.

A Dorling Kindersley Book

Troy of the Cowboys

Players in the National Football League (NFL) earn diamond-studded rings for winning the Super Bowl, the league's championship game. The game is played each year in January.

Many players play long careers without winning a Super Bowl ring.

Troy Aikman has won *three* Super Bowl rings!

Aikman, the popular, strong-armed quarterback of the Dallas Cowboys, has led his team to three Super Bowl championships.

This book tells the story of how Troy Aikman grew from being a little cowboy in a dusty Oklahoma town to being a Super Bowl-winning, Dallas Cowboy!

Moving around

Troy Kenneth Aikman was born in West Covina, California, on November 21, 1966. He grew up in Cerritos, a suburb south of Los Angeles.

Troy was a sports star from the first time he took the field. In Pop Warner football, he was a Junior All-America. He also played baseball and was one of the best players on his team.

Troy loved living in California. He had lots of friends to play with, the weather usually was nice, and they had lots of fun things to do.

Pop Warner
A major national youth football program is named for Glenn (Pop) Warner, a great coach at several colleges from 1895-1938.

But when Troy was 12, his family moved to a tiny town in Oklahoma called Henryetta.

"It was a big change for me," he said.

"I was used to living in a place where I could ride my bike all over," Troy said. "Now we were seven miles out of town on dirt roads. It was hard."

Troy made new friends, and sports continued to be an important part of his life. But he could play sports only after he had finished his chores. The Aikmans had moved to a working ranch, and there was always work to do.

Troy hauled hay for the horses. He helped feed the cows. While his friends back in California were going to the beach, Troy was working.

In Pop Warner football, Troy was a junior All-America.

But once the chores were done, it was time to play. And in a small Oklahoma town like Henryetta, the sport everyone loved most was football.

Aikman became the quarterback on the Henryetta High School team.

The quarterback is the leader of a football team's offense. The quarterback helps choose what plays his team runs. He also has a strong throwing arm and is a good runner.

Troy was a strong leader. He was a great passer and had good speed and moves as a runner. He became one of the top quarterbacks in the state.

In Troy's junior year, the team had a record of 2 wins and 8 losses, but Henryetta stuck by Troy and the team.

"The way our playoff system worked, the two games we had won put us into the state playoffs," Aikman said. "The way the town reacted, you would have thought we were unbeaten.

"Well, we got beat in the first round, but it was a fun ride."

Troy was such a sports fan, his birthday cake looked like a football field.

The kid from California became a hero in Henryetta. But he was loved in his adopted hometown not just because he was a football star—though that helped. Troy became a part of Henryetta because he was a nice, kind, hard-working young man.

Aikman continued to play football and improve his game. Soon he would finish high school...and look ahead to college.

His great skills on the field attracted attention from the biggest colleges in America. Coaches tried to recruit him for their schools. Troy had a big decision to make.

He thought he had made up his mind, but one final trip suddenly changed all that.

"I was all set to go to Oklahoma State," Aikman said. "But then I took a trip to Oklahoma University [O.U.]."

That trip changed his mind. The O.U. Sooners always had powerful teams, and were often in the hunt for the national championship.

The coaches and players really wanted Troy to play football with them. At a big banquet, Troy met many former Oklahoma stars.

The little kid from Henryetta was convinced. Oklahoma is for me, he thought. He agreed to go to O.U.

Oklahoma Sooners

The Oklahoma territory was opened to settlers on April 22, 1889. Some people crossed the line early and were called "Sooners."

Sooners, then Bruins

The thrill Aikman felt at the start of his college days soon turned bad. The coaches at Oklahoma broke a promise.

Instead of passing the ball often, which Troy loved to do, the Sooners decided to use the running attack they had used for years. Troy rarely played, and when he did, it was no fun.

"I was a tackling dummy there," he said. "I ran the ball all the time and was just getting blasted."

Aikman had a decision to make. Should he stay at Oklahoma, where he wasn't happy? Or should he try to change schools, and look for one where he could better use his talented arm?

In 1986, he made his decision.

He returned to his native California.

Troy was a strong, accurate passer in college.

Troy transferred to the University of California at Los Angeles (better known as UCLA). UCLA's teams are called the Bruins.

Although he had lived in California until he was 12, moving back to that state was another challenge.

"I had been away so long, I had become more used to Oklahoma," he said.

"It took me a while to adjust. And I could hardly ever wear my cowboy boots."

But he could wear his cleats. Aikman became the starter as a junior, his third college season and first at UCLA.

"Troy has all the ability to be a great player," UCLA coach Terry Donahue said. "He has size, arm strength, courage, and intelligence."

Under Troy's leadership, UCLA was 10-2 in 1987, and defeated Florida in the Aloha Bowl, a special postseason game held in Hawaii.

Football cleats

Football players wear leather shoes with hard plastic "cleats" or studs on the bottom for better traction.

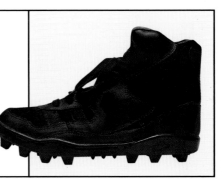

Troy's senior season in college was even better. He threw 24 touchdown passes, and UCLA again finished with a record of 10 wins and 2 losses.

The Bruins defeated Arkansas in the Cotton Bowl to cap off Troy's college career. Troy was named to the All-America team. He also won the Davey O'Brien Award as the nation's top college quarterback.

In deciding to leave Oklahoma and go to UCLA, Troy had made an important change in his life, and it had paid off.

Davey O'Brien
O'Brien (8) was a great quarterback at Texas Christian University from 1936 to 1938. He also played three years in the NFL.

"Without a doubt, the decision to go to UCLA put me in the position I'm in," Aikman says today about his NFL success.

In 1989, Aikman finished his college career. The next stop for the kid from Henryetta was the National Football League.

Troy helped the Bruins win the 1989 Cotton Bowl, held in Dallas, Texas.

He's number one

The Dallas Cowboys had the first pick in the 1989 NFL draft. The once-powerful team had finished 3-13 the year before. But the Cowboys had a new coach, Jimmy Johnson, and a new owner, Jerry Jones.

On April 23, they got their new quarterback: Troy Aikman.

The Cowboys made Troy the first player chosen in the draft, the league's annual selection of college players. Dallas gave Troy a big contract to be their starting quarterback.

Life in the NFL was very different for Troy than life in college. Football was a job now, and men were depending on him to come through. The pressure was on Troy.

The NFL Draft

NFL teams select college players at this annual event. Teams pick in reverse order of how they finished the previous year.

He had a rough rookie season in 1989. The team was young and didn't have a lot of great players. In the fourth game, Troy broke his finger and couldn't play for six weeks.

When he returned, the team had not gotten better. At the end of the season, the Cowboys were 1-15.

"That season was the worst," Troy said some years later.

"I dreamed so long to be an NFL quarterback, but nothing went right. My dream turned into a nightmare."

Things improved in 1990. Running back Emmitt Smith joined the team, along with other top young players.

With a broken finger, Troy could only watch from the sidelines.

With a year in the NFL under his belt, Troy was ready to lead the Cowboys back to the top.

Aikman and the Cowboys opened the 1990 season with a victory over San Diego. Troy scored his first NFL touchdown on a short run.

Troy led the Cowboys to an important victory over the Giants in 1991.

The rest of that season was up and down for Troy and Dallas. The team posted some big wins and some disappointing losses. But a final record of 7-9 showed that the team had improved.

In 1991, the improvement continued. Troy led the team to an important victory over the New York Giants, who had won the Super Bowl the season before.

"We needed to beat this team to establish ourselves," Troy said after the game.

With his pinpoint passing and field leadership, Troy was becoming one of the NFL's stars. Following the 1991 season, he was named to his first Pro Bowl, the NFL's all-star game.

Troy led the Cowboys over the 49ers; next stop, Super Bowl XXVII.

NFC and AFC

The NFL is made up of the American Football Conference (AFC) and National Football Conference (NFC).

As the 1992 NFL season began, the Cowboys had turned from one of the league's worst teams to one of the best.

Dallas stormed through the season with a 13-3 record, the most victories in club history. Troy passed for 3,445 yards, second best in the National Football Conference (NFC).

The Cowboys and the San Francisco 49ers played in the NFC Championship Game. The winner of that game would advance to Super Bowl XXVII in Pasadena, California.

The game was close until the third quarter. Troy led the Cowboys on a long drive that ended with a touchdown. Dallas never trailed again and won 30-20. The Oklahoma kid was about to play in the biggest game in sports.

In Super Bowl XXVII, Dallas faced the AFC-champion Buffalo Bills. The Bills were playing in their third consecutive Super Bowl and would provide a real test for the Cowboys.

Troy and the Cowboys passed the test with flying colors.

The Cowboys scored the second-most points ever in Super Bowl XXVII.

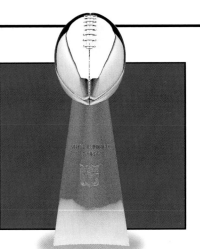

Lombardi Trophy
The Lombardi Trophy is awarded to the Super Bowl champion. It is named for Vince Lombardi, the legendary Packers coach.

The Dallas offense was in high gear, while the defense shut down the Bills.

The final score was Dallas 52, Buffalo 17. In only three seasons, the Cowboys had gone from the bottom of the NFL to the top.

Troy passed for 273 yards and four touchdowns in the game. After owner Jerry Jones accepted the Lombardi Trophy, Troy was called to the podium.

"And here he is, ladies and gentlemen," the television announcer said. "Troy Aikman, Super Bowl XXVII's most valuable player!"

Troy's success in the Super Bowl made him a national celebrity. He appeared on late-night talk shows and in commercials. He and the Cowboys went to the White House to meet President Bill Clinton.

Not long after Troy won his first Super Bowl ring, he went back home to Henryetta to see his old friends.

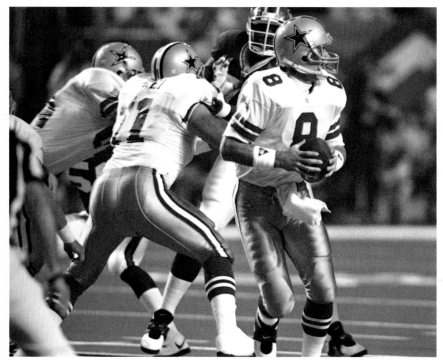

Two in a row! Troy and the Cowboys won their second NFL title in 1993.

He thanked them for supporting him when he was young by donating a new fitness center and college scholarships.

The town thanked him by naming a street after him.

"Having the folks in my hometown think that much of me was a real honor," Troy said.

In 1993, Troy had another Pro Bowl season. Emmitt Smith ran wild, and receivers Michael Irvin and Alvin Harper were among the NFL's best.

In Super Bowl XXVIII, Dallas faced Buffalo again. The final score was 30-13. Once again, the Dallas Cowboys were the champions of the NFL.

Still going strong

After the 1993 season, Dallas coach Jimmy Johnson left the team. The new coach of the Cowboys was Barry Switzer. Troy and the new Cowboys coach knew each other well.

Switzer had been the coach at Oklahoma whose style of play had resulted in Troy leaving to go to UCLA.

Troy with Coach Johnson...   *...and with Coach Switzer.*

Reporters always had a lot of questions for the leader of the Cowboys.

Would a new coach disrupt the Cowboys' successful team?

Troy's skills on the field would continue to be the key to the team's success. But just as important, he had matured into a team leader off the field.

"There is a lot of pressure, but there is pressure on all of us," Troy said.

Dallas overcame the pressure to win the NFC Eastern Division for the third year in a row. They faced the San Francisco 49ers for a spot in the Super Bowl.

But the Cowboys did not make it to the Super Bowl.

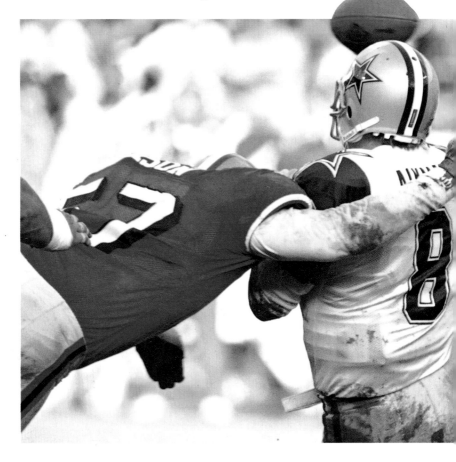

Troy passed for 380 yards and two touchdowns, but Dallas lost 38-28, and their Super Bowl streak was over.

Was Troy disappointed?

"Not at all," he said. "Our 1994 season was a success, even though we didn't make the Super Bowl."

In 1995, Dallas was second to none once more. Troy continued to be one of the best quarterbacks in the league.

Along with his leadership, Troy's greatest skill was his accuracy. He threw only seven interceptions in 1995, and was second in the NFC in completion percentage.

The Cowboys again were NFC East champions in 1995 with a 12-4 record. They advanced to Super Bowl XXX.

Interception
An interception happens when a defensive player catches a pass thrown by the opposing quarterback.

The field at the Super Bowl is decorated with team colors and league logos.

In Sun Devil Stadium in Arizona (above), the Cowboys faced the Pittsburgh Steelers. The Steelers' defense would give the Cowboys their toughest Super Bowl battle yet.

Dallas jumped out to a 13-7 lead in the first half, but Pittsburgh held firm in the third quarter.

Later, the Steelers scored twice to cut Dallas's lead to 20-17. Pittsburgh got the ball back with just over four minutes remaining in the game. If they scored a touchdown, would that end the Cowboys' chance for three Super Bowl victories?

As Troy watched from the sidelines, the Dallas defense came through. Larry Brown intercepted a Pittsburgh pass. Dallas scored another touchdown soon after on an Emmitt Smith run.

The Cowboys won 27-17 to earn their third Super Bowl championship in four years.

Troy depends on his offensive linemen to give him time to pass.

Since that 1995 season, the Cowboys have not returned to the Super Bowl. They have reached the playoffs three times, but have not advanced to the big game.

Troy Aikman is still one of the greatest quarterbacks in the game. He has earned six selections to the Pro Bowl (right). He holds Dallas records for most passing yards, attempts, and completions.

The Cowboys finished 8-8 in 1999 and made the playoffs. Troy and the Cowboys are still going strong.

"I'm very happy where I am now," he said before the 1999 season. "This is a good time professionally and personally. But I want to win a Super Bowl as much today as I did before our first one.

"I still feel like my best years are ahead of me."

Dallas Cowboys players, and the team's fans around the world, are happy to hear that.

A hero off the field

One of the best things about being a football hero is that you can help other people.

Troy has used his football celebrity to help in many different ways. He sponsors scholarships for students at Henryetta High School and UCLA. He lends his name and time to charitable groups in Texas. Many of the causes he is involved with help children.

Troy has helped the Make-A-Wish Foundation, which helps seriously ill children enjoy special events. He has also appeared in commercials that help the American Cancer Society, Easter Seals, and the United Way (left).

Troy's favorite way to help people is through the Troy Aikman Foundation. In 1995, the Foundation opened Aikman's End Zone (below) at Dallas Children's Hospital.

One of the coolest things in Aikman's End Zone is the Starbright World computer game. Kids at the hospital can use the Internet to talk with a cartoon Troy or with other kids in hospitals around the country. The End Zone also has a giant football helmet in which kids can sit while they read books.

Troy also spends some of his free time e-mailing his many friends and fans.

Troy enjoys auto racing. He drove this minicar in a race in Texas.

Being famous means having some special fun. Troy has acted in several television shows. And he has also sung country songs on a couple of CDs.

But whether he is helping raise money for kids or throwing touchdown

passes, Troy Aikman continues to be a champion, on and off the field.

Glossary

Contract
NFL players sign these agreements to play for their team in return for money.

Cotton Bowl
Held each New Year's Day, this postseason college football game matches two of the top teams in the nation.

Interception
When a defensive player catches a pass intended for an offensive player.

Most valuable player (MVP)
The best player in a game or during a season.

National Football League
The 31 professional football teams are divided into the American and National Football Conferences.

Playoffs
After the NFL season, the top 12 teams meet in a series of games to determine the league champion.

Pro Bowl
The NFL's annual postseason all-star game, held each February in Honolulu, Hawaii.

Quarterback
The most important position on a football team's offense; often calls plays, makes passes.

Running attack
Football teams move the ball by passing or running. The running attack describes the ways the teams run the ball.

Running back
Offensive football position that plays behind quarterback; takes handoffs and runs; also catches passes.

Scholarships
Top athletes or students have their school fees paid for by the college or a charity.

Super Bowl
The NFL's annual championship game, played each January at a neutral site between the champions of the AFC and the NFC.

Touchdown pass
When a quarterback throws the ball to a receiver in the end zone, or when a receiver catches a pass and then runs into the end zone.